Mother TERESA

Biography®

Mother TERESA

Amy Ruth

A&E®

Lerner Publications Company
Minneapolis

This book is dedicated to my niece, Miranda Rose, who came into this world a week before Mother Teresa left it. May you grow up as strong, confident, and happy as she was.

Lerner Publications Company
241 First Avenue North
Minneapolis, MN 55401

Website address: www.lernerbooks.com

Library of Congress Cataloging-in-Publication Data

Ruth, Amy.
    Mother Teresa / by Amy Ruth.
      p. cm. — (A & E biography)
    Includes bibliographical references and index.
    Summary: A biography of the nun who founded the order known as "The Missionaries of Charity" to work with the sick and destitute in Calcutta and other places and who was awarded the Nobel Peace Prize in 1979.
    ISBN 0-8225-4943-3 (alk. paper)
    1. Teresa, Mother, 1910–1997—Juvenile literature. 3. Nuns—India—Biography—Juvenile literature. [1. Teresa, Mother, 1910–1997. 2. Nuns. 3. Missionaries of Charity. 4. Women—Biography.] I. Title. II. Series.
BX 4406.5.Z8R87 1999
271'.97—dc21
[b]   98-23315

Manufactured in the United States of America
1 2 3 4 5 6 – JR – 04 03 02 01 00 99

CONTENTS

Young Agnes learned to pray, love her neighbors, and serve God from her mother, Drana Bojaxhiu.

Chapter **ONE**

AGNES

AGNES GONXHA BOJAXHIU TROTTED ALONGSIDE HER mother, Drana, as they made their way through the cobbled streets of Skopje, a town in southeastern Europe. The two walked past the corner street vendors and artisans and into the city's poorest neighborhoods, where young Agnes learned her first lessons in charity. Many poor peasants lived in Skopje (SKOP-yay) and in villages on the surrounding plains. Some of these people lacked enough money to buy food. Agnes and her mother gave out food, medicine, clothes, and money to the poor. Sometimes the mother-daughter pair cared for a sick widow who couldn't look after her six children. On other days they tended an elderly woman named File, who lived alone and had no one to see to her needs. Drana told Agnes that serving the poor was a way to serve God.

By the time Agnes was a senior in high school, she had decided to devote herself to God and follow his will for her. She joined a convent, and her work took her into India's worst slums. Here, she eventually became the world-renowned and beloved Mother Teresa, who worked among the world's poorest people, carrying out her mission of charity in the name of God.

Agnes Gonxha Bojaxhiu (bo-ya-JEE) was born on August 26, 1910, in Skopje, a town in Macedonia. Macedonia was a region in the Balkan Peninsula, also called the Balkans, in southeastern Europe. The Balkans were a melting pot of cultures, traditions, and languages. Turks, Greeks, Italians, Albanians, Serbs, and other ethnic groups lived throughout the peninsula. The Bojaxhiu family was Albanian, as were most of Skopje's residents.

Baby Agnes Gonxha (Gonxha [GOHN-jeh] means "flower bud" in Albanian), had a four-year-old sister, Age (AH-geh), and a seven-year-old brother, Lazar. The children and their parents lived comfortably in a large house surrounded by a flower garden and many fruit trees. By Balkan standards, the family was well off.

Agnes's father, Nikola Bojaxhiu, was a successful, self-made businessman who owned a construction company and imported luxury foods, including oil and sugar. Nikola, often called Kole, was known throughout the region for his generous donations to individuals, families, and institutions. He often gave money to the Church of the Sacred Heart, the Catholic church his family attended almost daily. Kole had once helped pay for the construction of Skopje's first theater, and he had served on the local town council.

Agnes's father spoke many languages and often traveled throughout the region and to exotic places such as Italy and Egypt. The Bojaxhius all spoke the Albanian, Macedonian, and Serbo-Croatian languages. Upon his return from his business trips, Kole always arrived with gifts for his children. But more than presents,

Agnes's father, Kole Bojaxhiu, valued family, hard work, and faith above all else.

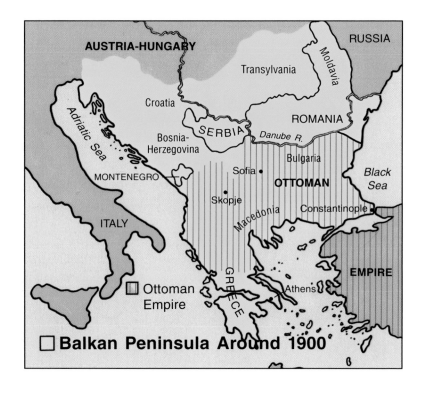

Agnes, Age, and Lazar awaited the stories Kole told of his travels.

Agnes's mother, Dranafile Bernaj Bojaxhiu, ran the household and cared for the children. Dranafile, often called Drana, was a deeply religious woman who was known in town for her charitable works toward Skopje's poor people. Besides walking the streets giving out badly needed supplies, Drana made sure that those who came to the Bojaxhiu door in search of food never left empty-handed.

When family friends gathered at the Bojaxhiu home, the house rang with stories, music, songs, and laughter. Agnes's father was an accomplished musician who played in a local brass band and enjoyed singing. He took great pride in his Albanian heritage and passed this sentiment on to his children, telling them never to forget whose children they were and what background they came from. The family dressed in brightly colored traditional folk costumes when they celebrated Albanian holidays and festivals. "We were a very happy family," Agnes said. "We lived for each other and we made each other's lives very full and very happy."

Agnes and her older brother had a special bond even though their personalities were very different. Agnes was a serious, hard-working girl who rarely got into trouble, while Lazar was often lazy and mischievous. Agnes polished Lazar's shoes and helped him with his household chores so he would not get into trouble. Their mother would tell Lazar, "Follow Agnes's example, even though she is younger than you." Agnes would stop her pantry-raiding older brother from eating after midnight, which was forbidden if the family was going to receive Communion in church the next day. She didn't tattle on him but in her own gentle way helped Lazar overcome his weakness.

Agnes also had a special relationship with her mother. "My mother was a holy woman," Agnes said. "She brought us up very closely, in the love of Jesus. She herself prepared us for our first communion, and so we learned to love God above all things from our Mother."

It was Agnes, more than her siblings, who followed in her mother's footsteps to care for Skopje's poor people. On days when Drana was busy at home, Agnes would venture out alone. The sensible Agnes took her mission very seriously.

Agnes, Age, and Lazar attended a Catholic elementary school. Their father, a strict disciplinarian, demanded obedience and good behavior from his children and expected them to excel in school. Often in the evenings, Agnes, Lazar, and Age would answer questions about what they had learned in school that day. Kole was an unusual Albanian father since he believed that his daughters should be fully educated and prepared for careers. Many Albanians in the early twentieth century still believed that education was wasted on women, since most would end up working as wives and mothers. Agnes thought maybe one day she would become a teacher or a writer.

Traditional Albanian costumes, like those above, were a common sight in the Bojaxhiu household.

During Agnes's childhood, Skopje had only a small Catholic population; most residents were Muslim. Muslims follow the teachings of the prophet Mohammed and worship the god Allah. Because of their small number, the Catholics of Skopje were closely united, and like the Bojaxhius, their lives centered around the church.

Skopje, like other Balkan towns, had a violent history. For hundreds of years, different ethnic and religious groups throughout the Balkans had fought one another for territory. By the end of the 1400s, the powerful Turkish Ottoman Empire occupied most of the Balkans, which the Turks ruled for more than four

Soldiers train for combat in the First Balkan War, which ended hundreds of years of Turkish rule.

hundred years. The Turks were Muslim, and they converted many Christians to this religion. People all over the Balkans, including Albanians, wanted to gain independence from the Turks.

In 1912, when Agnes was two years old, the Greeks, Serbs, Bulgarians, and Montenegrins finally defeated the Turks in what was called the First Balkan War. As a result, the Ottoman Empire's hold on the Balkans crumbled. Macedonia and other Balkan regions were divided into new countries. Albania became an independent country. Unfortunately for the Albanian Bojaxhius, Skopje fell outside the new Albanian boundaries and became part of Serbia.

Agnes's father had long been active in a movement for an independent Albania. Determined to get his home into Albanian territory, he joined a group dedicated to getting Skopje and neighboring towns into the new Albanian nation.

Throughout Agnes's childhood, fighting and unrest in the Balkans continued. In 1914, the First World War began, and people living in the Balkans experienced food shortages and bloodshed. To make matters worse, the Bojaxhius and other Albanians, especially Catholics, were under constant threat of attack by the Serbs, who despised both Albanians and Catholics.

Even though she was often afraid for her family, Agnes held firm to what her mother had taught her—that all people were created in, and deserved, God's love.

Agnes's brother, Lazar, said that his sister, second from left, **was a very solemn and earnest girl.**

Chapter **TWO**

THE FIRST CALL

THE BOJAXHIU FAMILY DREW ON ITS FAITH IN **1918,** when the strong and healthy Kole died unexpectedly. He had attended a political dinner in Belgrade, a city 160 miles from the Bojaxhiu home, to show his support for an independent and free Albania. He returned home gravely ill and soon died. Kole's fellow patriots and the Bojaxhius believed that Kole may have been poisoned because of his political beliefs.

While Agnes and her family grieved, Skopje's residents, both Catholic and Muslim, mourned the loss of such a fine man. On the day of his funeral, shops closed, and schoolchildren were given handkerchiefs as a sign of mourning. Many of the region's most influential citizens attended Kole's funeral.

Agnes was about seven years old when her father died, and the family, once quite well off, found itself worrying about money. Kole's business partner took over Kole's share of the business, leaving Agnes and her mother and siblings with only a place to live.

For a short time, Agnes felt like she had lost both of her parents. She watched as grief drained her mother of energy. Not only did Drana lose the man she loved, but she was left to deal with all the things that Kole had once taken care of, such as the family's finances and disciplining the children. For a few weeks, Agnes's thirteen-year-old sister tried to run the household.

Then, renewed by her faith, Drana mustered her strength. She had to be strong for her children—to make sure their needs were met. Agnes's mother decided that under no circumstances were her children going to be deprived of food, shelter, clothing, and education. She began to take in sewing and developed a handcrafted embroidery business. She made exquisite wedding dresses, festival costumes, rugs, and other finery. The Bojaxhius's reputation in Skopje helped Drana's business prosper.

During this difficult period in their lives, Agnes, Lazar, and Age grew even closer to one another. They learned to rely even more on their faith. The family gathered every evening to say the Rosary by reciting prayers to the Virgin Mary.

Drana resumed her husband's strict disciplinary practices. One evening, when the three children were romping in the living room, Drana got up from her chair and turned off the lights, plunging the room into darkness. She told the children if they weren't going to do something worthwhile with their time, they might as well sit in the dark.

Following Kole's death, Agnes grew even closer to her mother. Together, they became more religious. Agnes and her mother seemed to live as much in church as at home. Agnes helped her mother organize church festivals, feasts, and events such as plays, pageants, and concerts. They decorated the church with colorful flowers, garlands, and flags. More and more, Agnes began to associate good times with the activities of the church and with worshipping God.

The highlight of each year for Agnes was the pilgrimage she and her family made to worship at the shrine of the Madonna of Letnice in Montenegro, a country northwest of Skopje. At the feet of the revered Madonna and child statue, they prayed and their faith was replenished. For many Europeans, such pilgrimages were an important way to express their faith. Many of Skopje's Catholic residents made the trip every year, often traveling in groups as they walked or rode in horse-drawn carriages across the mountains. For many, like the Bojaxhius, the pilgrimage was the most important event of the year besides Christmas.

The trip was especially important for Agnes who suffered from colds, coughs, and other ailments that weakened her. She and Age often went to the shrine a

Agnes spent some of the happiest times of her childhood at the Madonna of Letnice shrine, high in the mountains of Montenegro, a neighboring country.

few weeks before the annual pilgrimage to rest and restore Agnes's health. They took long walks in the mountains and breathed the fresh country air along the Letnice River. Agnes liked to pray alone in the local church. When Drana, Lazar, and other Catholics eventually joined them in Letnice, everyone gathered around the hearth in the evenings to tell stories and play games. After Agnes made her annual visit to the shrine, her soul felt nourished with the love of God and Agnes would regain her health. The health and happiness she and her family felt there were enough to fuel them for the rest of the year.

One day when Agnes was twelve years old, she knelt at the feet of the Madonna and child statue. With a lighted candle in her hand, Agnes prayed to God. At that moment, Agnes first heard the call of God. "I heard the voice of God calling me to be all his by consecrating myself to him and to the service of my neighbors. . . . I was singing in my heart, full of joy inside. It was then that I realized that my vocation was for the poor."

Fourteen-year-old Agnes, right, *with Age,* left, *and Lazar,* center

Chapter **THREE**

JOY LIKE A COMPASS

FOR SIX YEARS AFTER SHE HEARD THE CALL AT THE Madonna of Letnice, Agnes threw herself into school and church activities. But God's calling was always in the back of her mind. Although she had been raised to accept the will of God without question, Agnes had doubts. Was the call genuine? What did God expect her to do?

Agnes believed answering her call from God meant becoming a nun, or a woman who is part of a religious order and who typically has taken vows of poverty, chastity, and obedience. She would have to give up the only life and the only home she had ever known, to travel into the unknown. She would be separated from her family and forced to give up any hope of marrying and having children. Her life would be hard, and she would not have access to the comforts she had grown up with.

In her teen years, Agnes was a good student at the local public schools. She was well organized, efficient, and extremely disciplined. Agnes tutored classmates who struggled through their lessons, and she taught younger children about Catholicism. Working with peers and children fulfilled Agnes. She cheerfully participated in social activities, especially church-related ones, with her friends.

Agnes respected people of different cultures and religions, believing that everyone worshipped the same God who was simply known by different names. She helped anyone in need, whether they were Albanian, Turkish, Greek, Italian, or any other nationality. Fluent in several languages, she often served as an interpreter for parish priests, translating Serbo-Croatian into Albanian.

Agnes and Age sang in the church choir, Agnes as a soprano and Age as an alto. Known as the church nightingales, the sisters also performed monthly charity concerts with the Albania Catholic Choir, often singing solos. Agnes's cousin Lorenz Antoni taught her to play the mandolin, a small stringed instrument resembling a guitar. "She learned quickly and became a good player," he said.

Agnes was quiet and contemplative. She loved to write poetry and would share her poems with friends.

She often carried a notebook with her, to be prepared when meaningful words came to her. A talented writer, she published two articles in the local newspaper. Her favorite pastime was reading. It was not unusual for her to curl up for hours with a book. Sometimes Drana warned Age and Lazar not to leave their younger sister alone for too long, or else she would read the day away.

When Agnes was fourteen, her brother won a scholarship to a school in Austria. Because the school was far away, Lazar saw his family only during school vacations. Age studied economics at a local college.

Since her father's death, Agnes had looked to the parish priests for a father figure. The year that Lazar

Agnes, second from right in the second row, *sometimes sang solos in her church choir.*

left, a new parish priest, Father Jambrenkovic, was named pastor of the Church of the Sacred Heart.

The new pastor was enthusiastic and dedicated to expanding and strengthening the church. His parishioners—young and old—were swept up in his enthusiasm. Soon, he was well loved by his congregation.

Father Jambrenkovic had a talent for organization, and he created a church library where Agnes spent many hours absorbed in religious reading material. Agnes joined Father Jambrenkovic's new Christian girls' society, the Sodality of the Blessed Virgin Mary, where girls studied the lives of saints and missionaries. The girls collected money to aid missionaries serving in India and other developing countries around the world, and prayed for them in small prayer groups they had formed.

Agnes was especially interested in the missionaries in India. Catholic missionaries had had a long-standing presence there, beginning with the arrival of Portuguese missionaries in the early 1400s. As more and more Christians arrived in later centuries, they opened schools, hospitals, and churches, and they worked to convert Indians to Christianity.

Agnes pored over magazines, such as *Catholic Missions*, that depicted the lives of missionaries working in poverty-stricken areas of India. Photographs of starving families pulled at Agnes's heart. She read about the sick and dying people in the slums of India, including the suffering lepers.

Photographs of starving families in India deeply moved Agnes.

Leprosy, a contagious virus that affects the skin and nerves, mainly spread among the sick and malnourished citizens of India. Leprosy can rot fingers and toes and can deform other parts of the body with lesions and sores. Catholic missionaries wanted desperately to help the millions of people who had this disease.

Father Jambrenkovic regularly reminded his youth group that poor people and lepers needed help. When Jesuit priests who worked in India visited Skopje, Agnes attended their lectures and listened attentively.

Jesuits are members of an order, or religious community, within the Catholic Church. Agnes said, "They used to give us the most beautiful descriptions about the experiences they had with the people and especially the children in India."

As Agnes learned more and more about the missionaries in India, she thought she knew where God was calling her. Why else would he surround her with so many images and stories of India? She began to seriously consider becoming a nun and working for the poor in India. She turned to Father Jambrenkovic for guidance. Was she making the right choice, she wondered? "Joy that comes from the depths of your being is like a compass by which you can tell what direction your life should follow," Father Jambrenkovic told her. "One should follow this, even when one is venturing upon a difficult path."

This was the push Agnes needed. Her heart filled with love for God, Agnes began to prepare for her spiritual journey. At sixteen years of age, she attended intensive retreats at the Madonna of Letnice and other Catholic shrines. Agnes knew that serving God and others *did* fill her heart with joy. And so, at age seventeen, she made her final decision to become a nun and go to India. "From then on," she said, "I have never had the least doubt of my decision."

Father Jambrenkovic helped Agnes apply to the Loreto order, a Catholic order based in Ireland. The Loreto sisters had several missions throughout the world, including well-established missions in India, where the nuns taught school.

Agnes knew that if the Loreto order accepted her, her journey would take her far from home and she might never see her family again. In the early 1900s, Catholic nuns were not given vacations with family. The thought of forever separating from Drana, Age, and Lazar, filled her with sadness, but she said, "It was the will of God: he made the choice."

Agnes's mother had mixed feelings about her daughter's choice. When Agnes shared her decision with her mother, Drana shut herself in her bedroom for twenty-four hours, praying and thinking. The religious Drana certainly wanted Agnes to serve God. But like Agnes, Drana knew that they might never see each other again. When she emerged from her room she told Agnes, "Put your hand in His hand and walk all the way with Him."

Age was sad, too, but she also wanted Agnes to follow her heart. When Agnes told Lazar of her decision, he was angry. He did not understand why his bright and talented sister would choose a lifestyle that would obligate her to give up everything. Lazar, after attending a military academy in Tirana, a city in Albania, had just been appointed an officer in the army of King Zog I, who had just taken over most of Albania. Agnes explained her decision to her brother quite simply, "You will serve a king of two million people, I will serve the King of the whole world."

Agnes, just before leaving for the Loreto convent in Ireland

Chapter **FOUR**

BOUND FOR INDIA

A **LARGE GROUP OF FRIENDS AND CHURCH MEMBERS** gathered at the Bojaxhiu home to say farewell to Agnes. Members of Agnes's church pressed gifts into her hands and wished her well on her long journey. She would first go to Loreto Abbey in Dublin, Ireland, for several weeks, and then on to India. More than a going-away party, the festivities were a celebration of a young woman who had chosen to devote her life to God. The Church of the Sacred Heart held a special service for Agnes, and the choirs she had sung with held a musical concert in her honor. *Catholic Missions,* the magazine partly responsible for enticing Agnes to India, recorded her departure: "She was the life and soul of the Catholic girls' activities and the church choir, and it was generally acknowledged that her departure would leave an enormous gap."

On September 25, 1928, Agnes, Drana, and Age boarded a train headed for Zagreb, a city hundreds of miles north of Skopje. From Zagreb, Agnes would travel to Ireland. About a hundred friends gathered at the Skopje train station to say good-bye.

Lorenz Antoni wrote: "The train began to move. On the platform we stood waving our handkerchiefs, and she waved back as long as we could see her. The distant sunlight illuminated her briefly and she seemed to us like the moon slowly vanishing in the light of day; growing smaller and smaller, still waving, still vanishing. And then we saw her no more."

Agnes, Drana, and Age spent a few happy days together in Zagreb before Agnes bid them a tearful farewell at the train station. Agnes was joined by Betika Kajnc, a young woman also bound for the Loreto convent in Ireland. The two kept each other company during the long journey through Austria, Switzerland, France, and England, until they finally arrived at the Loreto Abbey in Rathfarnham, Ireland.

The Loreto Abbey was a simple building situated at the end of a tree-lined driveway. How different it was from Agnes's snug home in Skopje, where everything and everyone were familiar. At the abbey, Agnes shed her street clothes and donned the habit of the Loreto nuns, a flowing robe and a veil.

Agnes knew it would take several years to become a

Loreto nun. First she would be a postulant, or future nun; then, in India, she would enter her novitiate, a two-year period during which novices were introduced to the strictness of life in a religious order. After completing her novitiate, Agnes would take her first vows as a nun. At Loreto Abbey, she began to study English, the language in which Loreto nuns taught school in India. She also studied the history of the order.

The Loreto order was an Irish branch of an English order founded in 1609 by Mary Ward, a woman who wished to reform the life and work of Catholic nuns. For hundreds of years, nuns had been cloistered— required to live and work inside convent walls. Mary Ward wanted nuns to have more freedom to serve the poor. Her unorthodox requests created much controversy in the Catholic Church, and she was once imprisoned for her beliefs. She died not having achieved her goal, and nuns continued to be cloistered. Church officials did their best to erase Mary Ward's existence from the order's institutional history. No one spoke of her for decades, and it wasn't until the 1920s that the Loreto nuns rediscovered their original founder.

By the time Agnes arrived in Ireland, the Loreto nuns had been working in convents in India for almost ninety years. Their primary mission was teaching, and they were known as excellent educators of girls. Loreto convent schools, or schools inside convent walls, in Australia, South Africa, and India attracted mostly pupils from wealthy families who

Agnes, top row on the right, *poses with other nuns from Loreto.*

wanted their children to benefit from the British style of education and upbringing.

In November 1928, Agnes and Betika said good-bye to the Irish Loreto nuns and boarded the *Marcha,* setting sail for Calcutta, India. The seven-week trip took the postulants along the most direct route to India— through the Mediterranean Sea, the Suez Canal, the Red Sea, and finally, the Indian Ocean.

During their journey, Agnes and Betika were distressed because there was no Catholic priest aboard. Their travel companions included three other nuns and many Protestant passengers, but no one to give communion, say Mass, or hear confession. Even on Christmas Day, they had to celebrate without Mass. Instead, they said the Rosary, sang Christmas carols, and created an impromptu Nativity scene depicting the birth of Jesus. They held their services on the ship's deck as the moonlight reflected off the ocean waves.

Before the ship arrived in Calcutta, it briefly docked in Madras, a city in southeastern India. Here, Agnes got her first glimpse of the horrifying poverty that had called to her from the pages of *Catholic Missions* magazine. She recorded the event in letters published in *Catholic Missions:* "We were shocked to the depths of our beings by their indescribable poverty. Many families live in the streets, along the city walls, even in places thronged with people. Day and night they live in the open on mats they have made from large palm leaves—or, often, on the bare ground."

Many Loreto nuns described Sister Teresa, as Agnes came to be known, as ordinary, simple, and gentle.

Chapter **FIVE**

THE SISTERS OF LORETO

ON JANUARY 6, 1929, EIGHTEEN-YEAR-OLD AGNES
Bojaxhiu arrived—without fuss or fanfare—in Calcutta,
in the province of Bengal. She wrote to *Catholic Missions:* "When our ship docked, we sang a silent *Te
Deum.* On the quayside, our Indian sisters were waiting
for us, and with a joy I cannot describe, we touched
the soil of Bengal for the first time. . . . Pray for us
a great deal, that we may become good and courageous
missionaries."

In 1929, India was still a colony of the vast and
powerful British Empire. Calcutta was one of the
largest cities in India. It was a center of trade and
commerce, with fancy business and shopping districts.
Wealthy British families built magnificent homes and

social clubs in the residential areas. The city boasted breathtaking Hindu temples, and neighborhoods that exploded with color, texture, and lush tropical gardens.

But amidst Calcutta's luxury and prosperity, a crippling and squalid poverty gripped Indian peasants. Hundreds of thousands of people lived on the streets, driven from their rural homes by poverty, natural disasters, sickness, and famine.

Many of the poor were victims of India's Hindu caste system. Most of India's population practiced Hinduism, a religion whose followers worship several gods and believe in reincarnation, or continual

Due to the stark inequality between the rich and the poor, Calcutta became known as a city of contrasts.

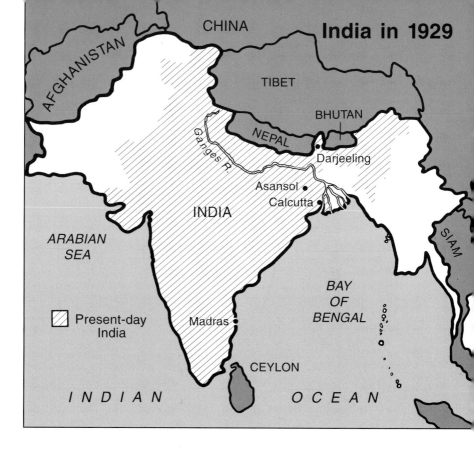

India in 1929

rebirth. Hindus believe that people are born into their "place" in society, and that place determines occupation, marriage, and social practices. Higher castes were assured good jobs and comfortable lives. Even lower than the lowest caste, the "Untouchables" lived in poverty and worked in the most menial jobs. Hindus could not change their castes, so lower caste members and Untouchables could not hope for a better life for themselves or their children. Only in their next life could they hope to be in a higher caste.

Hundreds of thousands of poor families thronged Calcutta's streets—living, cooking, and washing amidst litter and human and animal waste. Water for cooking, washing, and drinking usually mixed with waste from city latrines, creating breeding grounds for such diseases as smallpox, dysentery, and tuberculosis. Some people made huts and shacks of cardboard, bamboo, palm leaves, or other stray materials. Those who were not fortunate enough to have a dirty hovel to live in found space on the sidewalk or along gutters to call home. Many people survived by picking through mountains of garbage heaped along the city streets.

Bengal's intense weather added further pressure to the already burdened city of Calcutta. Between May and October, monsoons, storms with heavy rains and strong winds, raged throughout the region, sometimes causing landslides. Rainwater backed up the overflowing sewer systems, filling the streets with rivers of raw sewage.

Arriving in India in January, Agnes was greeted by pleasant weather, typical of the season. But by April and May, temperatures rose above one hundred degrees Farenheit with high humidity, making for sticky and uncomfortable living and working conditions. This was a shock for Agnes, who had grown up with mild summers and cold winters.

Agnes and Betika were first taken to the comfortable, spacious Loreto compound. The compound was near a large slum called Motijhil in Calcutta's eastern industrial district known as Entally. Loreto nuns and their students lived in the convent, sheltered from the surrounding slums. Because of the rule of enclosure, the nuns left the compound only for emergencies or annual spiritual retreats at another Loreto convent in Darjeeling, a beautiful mountain city four hundred miles north of Calcutta. Whenever a nun had to leave the convent grounds, she was accompanied by another nun, and they were driven to the train station or another destination in a private car.

After a week in the Calcutta convent, Agnes traveled by train to the Loreto convent in Darjeeling. There she began her novitiate. Agnes and the other novices were instructed in theology, prayer, and the Scriptures (the books of the Bible). Agnes began an intensive study of the Bengali and Hindi languages and continued her English lessons.

Since they were not yet nuns, the Loreto novices were allowed to work outside the convent. They taught in a local school for two hours each morning. In addition to teaching, Agnes was allowed to work in a small hospital, where she assisted doctors and tended to the physical and spiritual needs of desperately poor and malnourished patients.

In her letters to *Catholic Missions*, Agnes captured the scene of the hospital for her readers: "The tiny verandah is always full of the sick, wretched, and the miserable. All eyes are fixed, full of hope. . . . Many have come from a distance, walking for as much as three hours. What a state they are in! Their ears and feet are covered in sores. On their backs are lumps and lesions among the numerous ulcers." When

Loreto nuns and students picnic in the picturesque mountains surrounding Darjeeling, India, near the convent where Sister Teresa completed her novitiate.

doctors could offer no medicine or cure to a patient, Agnes gave a blessing.

A Jesuit priest, much like those who had enthralled Agnes with their tales of missionary work, sent home word of Agnes's and Betika's progress. "They are really happy and fulfilled," he wrote. "It's astonishing to me how healthy they seem to be. Already they are speaking English and Hindi well, and they are learning Bengali."

In May 1931, after two years as a novice, Agnes took her first vows as a Loreto nun. As was the custom, she lay flat on her stomach during much of the ceremony to symbolize her decision to give herself wholly and completely to God and to observe the vows of poverty, chastity, and obedience. She adopted a new name—Sister Teresa—after the patron saint of missions, Thérèsa of Lisieux. As her namesake had done, Sister Teresa pledged to wholeheartedly submit to the will of God. She believed that God would always show her what to do and would give her the tools with which to carry out his work.

With the novitiate behind her, twenty-year-old Sister Teresa returned to Calcutta to begin her new life at the Loreto convent where she had spent her first week in India.

Sister Teresa's childhood dream of teaching became a reality when she studied for her teaching certificate and was assigned to teach history and geography at two Loreto convent schools. Loreto Entally was a British-style school for wealthy Indian and British girls, and St. Mary's was a school for Bengali girls from various economic backgrounds. At St. Mary's, Sister Teresa taught in Bengali. Some of her students were poor and attended the school on scholarship.

Sister Teresa, like the other Loreto nuns, often worked as many as eighteen hours a day. The nuns rose before dawn to pray. During the week they taught school and supervised the students' recreation, study, and meal times. They also graded papers, got boarders off to bed, and led prayers and religious lessons in the evenings. It was an exhausting schedule, but Sister Teresa thrived, confident that she was doing God's work. "I can't say whether I was a good teacher," Sister Teresa said, "this my pupils know better. But I loved teaching."

Despite her schedule, Sister Teresa faithfully wrote letters home. By 1934, Drana and Age had left Skopje and were living with Lazar in Tirana. Political unrest continued in the Balkans. Although the family was mostly reunited, Drana missed Agnes. Still, Drana wrote that she was proud that her daughter was carrying out her vows so faithfully.

In 1935, twenty-five-year-old Sister Teresa was given an exemption from the rule of enclosure and assigned to teach at St. Teresa's, a school located outside the convent walls. Sister Teresa had a short walk to the school, which allowed her to move among the city's poor each day. Sheltered for four years from the poverty of the slums, she suddenly came face to face with the surrounding destitution. Her students were poor, and St. Teresa's facility was stark.

At first, Sister Teresa's students were shocked when she, a nun, cleaned the schoolroom. In India, only the lowliest citizens did such menial tasks. Soon the children began to help, and they transformed the classroom into a clean and tidy place. Within a few months, word had spread about the dedicated and friendly new teacher. Enrollment quickly doubled. Sister Teresa's students began calling her "Ma," or mother. Her new pupils came to love the spirited and dedicated teacher whose love and energy seemed to have no end.

Living in cramped and dirty hovels, many of St. Teresa's students were chronically ill, some suffering from tuberculosis, a lung infection that was often deadly. After touring the meager slum homes that surrounded the school, Sister Teresa knew why her students were so eager and happy to attend school. "When I first saw where the children slept and ate, I was full of anguish," Sister Teresa wrote. "It is not possible to find worse poverty. And yet, they are happy. Blessed children!"

In 1937, at the age of twenty-six, Sister Teresa took her final vows. She was as steadfast in her decision to serve God as she had been nine years before when she told her family that she had decided to become a nun. Almost immediately after she had taken her final vows, her superiors at the Loreto convent named her principal of St. Mary's convent school. They recognized that Sister Teresa was well liked by students, parents, and fellow nuns. The other Loreto nuns thought of her as a kind, ordinary person who worked hard and was completely devoted to God.

Her organizational skills and discipline served her well in her new position. She continued to teach history and geography, but her full-time commitment at St. Mary's kept her from St. Teresa's.

In the ten years since Sister Teresa had left Skopje, she had continued to develop an intense relationship with God, finding strength and purpose in work and worship. Life in the Loreto compound was comfortable and peaceful. "In Loreto I was the happiest nun in the world," she said.

Sister Teresa loved living and teaching at Loreto Entally, above, *and at St. Mary's. These schools were considered among the best in Calcutta.*

Chapter **SIX**

THE SECOND CALL

SISTER TERESA'S WORK WAS REWARDING, BUT AS each year passed, she grew further and further away from her calling to serve the poor. But though she was cut off from direct contact with the poor, Sister Teresa did have indirect contact through her students.

Some of the pupils at Loreto Entally and St. Mary's had joined the Sodality of the Blessed Virgin Mary, similar to the society Sister Teresa had joined as a girl. Under the direction of Father Julien Henry, one of Sister Teresa's spiritual advisors, the girls ventured into Calcutta's slums to tend to the poor. As much as Sister Teresa wanted to join them and resume the work she had done briefly at St. Teresa's, her superiors no longer permitted her to work outside the convent.

"She [Sister Teresa] asked us to gather them [the poor] around us, teach them the alphabet and some songs, and to make them happy," said Subhasini Das, a St. Mary's student. Sister Teresa had come to believe that the poor and the sick were closest to God—they were his chosen. She taught her pupils this, encouraging them to joyfully serve the poor as they would joyfully serve God.

The girls visited the sick in a nearby hospital and comforted families in the slums of Motijhil, just outside the convent walls. *Motijhil* means "Pearl Lake," but the name did not fit the image. In the 1930s, Motijhil was one of the poorest slums in Calcutta. When the girls returned from their trips, they would crowd around Sister Teresa, sharing what they had seen and done.

Outside the convent walls, India was undergoing major change. By 1939, the movement to free India from British colonization was becoming widespread. Mohandas Gandhi, the leader of the freedom movement, believed that the way to achieve this goal was through nonviolent protest. The Second World War began that year in Europe. Britain involved India by enlisting Indian soldiers and ordering food and other supplies from the Indian government, thus intensifying the already horrifying poverty within India.

The years 1942 and 1943 were especially difficult for India. A devastating flood and cyclone swept through the country, destroying much of Bengal's crops. The food that was produced was hoarded by the government to feed Indian and British troops still fighting in the Second World War. Hungry peasants from the countryside descended on Calcutta, looking for food. Although private charities and government organizations set up soup kitchens and other emergency relief stations, efforts were mostly too little too late. Over three million people died from starvation and disease during those two years.

Inside the convent, Sister Teresa, the other nuns, and the students were protected and supported by money and food donated by the Catholic Church. They saw little of the devastation surrounding them. They continued to teach, study, and pray for an end to the starvation.

In Albania, political unrest continued. Italy had occupied Albania, and Lazar joined the Italian army. In 1944, Communist revolutionaries took over Albania's government, and Lazar fled to Italy. The revolutionaries sealed off Albania, restricting travel in and out of the country. Still in Tirana, Drana and Age were prohibited from leaving.

By August 1946, conditions in Calcutta had worsened. The Second World War had ended, but a war of independence had erupted in India. As Indian citizens continued to demand freedom from the British, tension was mounting between the two largest religious groups in India, the Muslims and Hindus. Muslims, fearing a government ruled by Hindus, demanded their own country. Massive rioting and fighting between Hindus and Muslims ensued, and thousands of people died within days. Even the Loreto convent was affected by the events because supply trucks could not maneuver through the rioting. As principal, Sister Teresa watched St. Mary's food supply dwindle until there was nothing left. Desperate to find food for her pupils, she left the Loreto compound at one point and wandered the streets, seeing firsthand the terrible slaughter that had taken place. Everywhere she looked there were bodies of the dead and wounded.

In the fall of 1946, a month after she had walked through the aftermath of the civil strife, Sister Teresa's life was changed forever. Sick with what perhaps was tuberculosis, the thirty-six-year-old nun traveled to Darjeeling to recuperate. On the way, she experienced what she described as "a call within her call."

"It was on the tenth of September 1946, on the train that took me to Darjeeling, the hill station in the Himalayas, that I heard the call of God," she said. "In quiet, intimate prayer with our Lord, I heard distinctly, a call within a call. The message was quite clear: I was to leave the convent and help the poor whilst living among them. It was an order."

Upon her return, Sister Teresa consulted with her spiritual advisors, certain that she must follow God's calling. Following the call would mean breaking her sacred commitment to live her entire life in the Loreto order. Her advisors suggested that she petition to leave the Loreto convent to become a nun who could live and

Severe famine in the mid-1940s created an even greater need to help the poor.

work outside the convent walls. Her request required approval from various people and departments within the Catholic Church, including officials at the Loreto Abbey in Rathfarnham, Ireland, and Pope Pius XII, the head of the Catholic Church, in Vatican City.

Sister Teresa knew that obtaining this permission would be a struggle. Some of her superiors, including Archbishop Ferdinand Perier, the head of the Catholic Church in Calcutta, disapproved of her request. They did not like the idea of a nun living and working alone in the slums of Calcutta and warned Sister Teresa that she might have to give up her status as a nun.

A number of people supported Sister Teresa wholeheartedly, however. Father Celeste Van Exem, one of her spiritual advisors, petitioned on her behalf. "I was very impressed," he said of Sister Teresa's response to God's call. "From the beginning I had the feeling that it was a real vocation. . . . [She] was not an exceptional person, she was an ordinary Loreto nun." Father Van Exem believed that it was Sister Teresa's ordinariness that made her calling so pure and believable.

Sister Teresa patiently did what her advisors recommended, including writing the necessary letters to

Sister Teresa heard her second call while riding on the Calcutta-Darjeeling train.

Church officials. She was sent to work in the kitchen and gardens of a Loreto convent in Asansol, a city about three hundred miles northwest of Calcutta. Meanwhile, church officials discussed her situation. Throughout the difficult period of uncertainty, Sister Teresa held fast to her belief that God wanted her to continue her work as a nun—and perhaps found her own order.

After two long years of waiting and praying, the pope finally granted Sister Teresa permission to work for one year among the poor as a Loreto nun. After this probationary period, her church superiors would rule on whether she should continue to work outside the convent.

Although Sister Teresa knew that most people were pleased to see her follow her calling, others—including some of her students—were saddened. "We were very upset," one of her students said, "as all of us were deeply attached to her."

On August 16, 1948, thirty-seven-year-old Sister Teresa stepped through the gates of the Loreto convent to begin her new life. Dressed in a simple white sari (the dress of an Indian woman) bordered with blue stripes, Sister Teresa had a cross pinned to her shoulder, rough sandals on her feet, and a small sum of money given to her by the Loreto order.

" . . . [T]o leave Loreto was my greatest sacrifice," Sister Teresa said, "the most difficult thing I have ever done. It was much more difficult than to leave my family and country to enter religious life. Loreto meant everything to me."

Sister Teresa believed the poor were God's chosen people.

Chapter **SEVEN**

MOTHER TERESA

SISTER TERESA'S FIRST STEPS OUT OF THE LORETO convent took her 240 miles north of Calcutta to the city of Patna. Here, with the Medical Missionary Sisters who provided medical service to the poor, Sister Teresa spent four months learning as much as she could about medical first aid and nursing. She knew that the poor she would serve in Calcutta would require medical help. She observed operations and assisted in childbirth. By the time her training was complete, Sister Teresa had learned to prescribe medicine, give injections, and run a medical facility.

Throughout her stay, she sought advice from the order's mother superior, Mother Dengal. Years earlier Mother Dengal had asked for permission from church officials to found her own order where she could work directly with the poor. Sister Teresa declared that if she were to begin such an order, she and her nuns would eat only rice and salt, the diet of the poorest of the poor. Mother Dengal peered back at the younger nun and asked, "How do you expect your sisters to work, if their bodies receive no sustenance? The very poor work very little, become sick, and die young. Do you want your nuns to suffer the same fate?" Realizing that Mother Dengal was right, Sister Teresa agreed to keep herself and her helpers well fed, so that their strength and good health could be used to do God's work.

On December 21, 1948, Sister Teresa returned to Calcutta. Her divine call could not have come at a better time. The year before, India had finally been granted independence from Britain. India was split in two when a new Muslim nation, Pakistan, was created from lands in northwest and northeast India. Fighting and bloodshed again raged between the different religious groups. Fearing for their lives, Hindus who had been living in the newly formed Pakistan fled to India. Muslims fled to Pakistan. Again, hundreds of thousands of refugees descended on congested urban areas like Calcutta.

Following the advice of Father Van Exem, Sister Teresa took up residence with the Little Sisters of the Poor, a Catholic order of nuns located an hour's walk from the Motijhil slums, where she intended to begin her "real work." The Little Sisters ran St. Joseph's Home, a haven for elderly people.

In 1947, India became an independent Hindu nation and Pakistan became a Muslim nation. Thousands of Hindus and Muslims fled their former homes because they were afraid to stay in a country ruled by members of the other religion.

After a few days of rest, Sister Teresa felt she was ready to begin her work in Motijhil. She walked, alone and without a plan, toward the familiar Loreto convent and the slums that surrounded it. "I walked and walked . . . until I couldn't walk anymore," Sister Teresa said of her first day in the slums. "Then I understood better the exhaustion of the really poor, always in search of a little food, of medicines, of everything."

Each day she walked through the slums, looking for

ways to help what seemed like endless numbers of suffering people. Each night she returned exhausted and despairing. The task of helping all of the poor people lining the streets seemed insurmountable. But she hadn't wavered from her belief that God had provided her with strength and would lead her in the right direction.

Beginning with what was most familiar to her, Sister Teresa decided to start a school. She encouraged a few Motijhil families to let her teach their children. Eager youngsters who had had few or no opportunities to go to school flocked around her. Using the dirt as a blackboard and sticks as chalk, Sister Teresa opened her first school under Calcutta's blazing sun. The children's first lesson was the Bengali alphabet. Soon, as more and more students joined the school, the recitation of the alphabet could be heard in the nearby streets.

Sister Teresa also taught her students personal hygiene. She often gave them baths before beginning their lessons. With her meager funds from the Loreto convent, she bought bars of soap for her students, giving them as prizes for a well-learned lesson and good attendance. She also went into her students' homes, instructing parents in cleanliness and helping to clean their homes and clothes.

Sometimes, residents of Motijhil doubted Sister Teresa's intentions. Some did not believe that a European Catholic nun could live and work among the poor without trying to convert them to Christianity. During

Sister Teresa's first week in Motijhil, some residents threw stones at her and screamed at her to leave.

Many other residents supported her efforts. Impressed by her relentless energy and unbounded love for the poor, people who could afford to donate gave Sister Teresa money and supplies to do her work. Shortly after arriving in Motijhil, Sister Teresa applied for and was granted Indian citizenship, transforming the doubts of many skeptics into acceptance and admiration.

Two weeks after she had established her school in Motijhil, Sister Teresa received a large donation that allowed her to rent two rooms in a nearby building. She converted them into a schoolroom and a small medical facility. She taught school in the mornings and treated patients in the afternoons.

Attendance at the school rose steadily. More and more parents sent their children to her, intrigued by the nun's interest in the children's welfare. Within a few months, Sister Teresa had fifty-six students and three volunteer teachers from the community. The teachers taught reading, writing, math, and needlework.

In her makeshift clinic, Sister Teresa gave medicine and health care to poor people who lined up to see her. Volunteers, mostly women from the community and students from Loreto, helped Sister Teresa in the clinic. To obtain medicines and other medical supplies, Sister Teresa made what she called "begging trips" or wrote "begging letters" to pharmacies. Some people gave generously. Others surprised Sister Teresa with their unwillingness to help.

Sister Teresa spent every waking moment tending to the residents of Motijhil any way she could. She often gave away her busfare and the meager lunch she had brought with her from the Little Sisters' convent. She even ignored the advice of Mother Dengal and slept only a few hours a night.

With her school and clinic well underway in Motijhil, Sister Teresa directed her efforts on Tiljala, another slum district. By early 1949, she had established a school and clinic there. Her decision to branch out into another district while many Motijhil residents were still suffering drew criticism from many Motijhil residents. Trying to serve as many poor people in as many areas as possible, however, was quickly becoming a foundation of Sister Teresa's work philosophy.

Around the time she established her second school, in Tiljala, Sister Teresa began to look for a home where she could live closer to the slums in which she worked. In February 1949, with the help of Father Van Exem, Sister Teresa moved into a room in the house of Michael Gomes and his family. The home, at 14 Creek Road, was on a curvy road lined with homes and shops in a wealthy neighborhood near the slums.

The Gomeses were wealthy Christian Indians anxious to lend a hand to the woman who was doing so much for the poor in Calcutta. The family would not accept money for rent and often shared its food with

Sister Teresa, especially when she gave her own food away to the poor.

Upon moving into her room, Sister Teresa removed the comfortable and attractive furniture, preferring to keep only a bed and wooden boxes to use for a chair and table. Although she lived outside the walls of the Loreto convent, she did not forget her sacred vows, including her vow of poverty. She believed, more than ever, that if the poor could exist without luxuries such as furniture, curtains, and pretty clothes, they were not necessary in her own life.

Exhausted and living away from the comfortable daily life she had enjoyed inside the convent, Sister Teresa often felt lonely. She wrote in her diary, "God wants me to be a lonely nun laden with the poverty

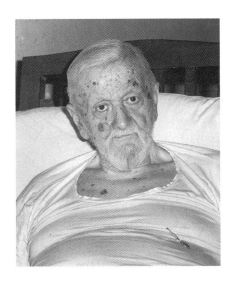

Father Celeste Van Exem, an ardent supporter of Sister Teresa and one of her spiritual advisors

of the cross. Today I learned a good lesson. The poverty of the poor is so hard. When I was going and going until my legs and arms were paining, I was thinking how they have to suffer to get food and shelter. Then the comfort of Loreto came to tempt me. But God, out of love for you, and by my own free choice, I desire to do whatever be your holy will. Give me courage now, this moment."

Sister Teresa, often accompanied by Michael Gomes's

Sister Teresa felt depressed and discouraged every night after seeing the hordes of poverty-stricken people living on the streets.

daughter, Mabel, continued making begging trips and writing begging letters to people or organizations who could donate medical or other supplies. Sister Teresa began to develop a reputation among Calcutta's city officials and influential citizens as a determined, aggressive, and compassionate humanitarian. Many found it hard to say "no" to the persistent nun who would sometimes wait for hours until a "no" turned into a "yes." Once, after a pharmacist had refused her plea for some free medicine to give to the poor, she waited for hours in his reception area until he was so distracted that he gave her the medicine simply to be rid of her. Sister Teresa was a small woman and stood barely five feet tall, but her presence was imposing and the impression she left on people was long lasting.

Toward the end of her year-long probationary period, Sister Teresa began to plan her next step. It was time to begin the process of founding her own religious order, in which nuns would be free to work outside the convent walls and whose life work would be to serve the poor. With help from her faithful supporter Father Van Exem and from Archbishop Perier, who was impressed with Sister Teresa's work, she wrote a constitution for this new order to be submitted to church officials for review. Again, Sister Teresa's request would require the approval of the pope.

Meanwhile, Sister Teresa's first postulants, mostly former students, began arriving at Creek Road. "They wanted to give everything to God, and they were in a hurry to do it," Sister Teresa said. The first to arrive was Subhasini Das, a former student and the daughter of wealthy Bengalis. More young women followed, ready to devote their lives to God and determined to work with Sister Teresa. She usually insisted, however, that the eager volunteers finish school first.

Soon, the entire third floor of the Gomes home was given over to Sister Teresa and her postulants. Not yet a religious order, Sister Teresa and her postulants still lived according to the rules of one, following a strict schedule of work, rest, prayer, and spiritual study. They began their day with prayers and a church service at four-thirty. They spent the rest of the morning working among poor people. Often, in their desperate efforts to feed the poor, they would take tin cups door to door around Calcutta's more prosperous neighborhoods, asking for leftover food scraps. They returned to Creek Lane for lunch and a short nap, followed by more service to the poor, dinner, prayers, and bedtime by ten o'clock. "Our community is very closely woven together," Sister Teresa said. "We do everything together: we pray together, we eat together, we work together."

October 1950 marked a turning point in the life of the forty-year-old Sister Teresa. The pope approved the founding of a new order, the Missionaries of Charity, with Sister Teresa as mother superior. Now called Mother Teresa, her order had officially become part of the Catholic Church. "I didn't choose this name

Missionaries of Charity," Mother Teresa said. "It came from the call. It is what we are meant to be: carriers of God's love."

The event was celebrated at a special mass where ten of Mother Teresa's postulants began their official novitiates. Out of respect and love for her teacher, Subhasini Das took the name Sister Agnes. The young women took the original three vows of chastity, poverty, and obedience. It was the fourth vow—"To give wholehearted and free service to the poorest of the poor"—that set them apart from other orders. "The Missionaries of Charity do firmly believe that they are touching the body of Christ in his distressing disguise whenever they are helping and touching the poor," Mother Teresa said of the fourth vow. By accepting the fourth vow, the young women pledged to serve the poor, the sick, and the dying without hesitation.

Mother Teresa said, "Missionaries of Charity must be healthy of mind and body. [Each nun] must have ability to learn. She must have plenty of common sense and a cheerful disposition."

Chapter EIGHT

MISSIONARIES OF CHARITY

BY **1953,** THE **MISSIONARIES** OF **CHARITY** HAD outgrown the third floor of Michael Gomes's home on Creek Lane, and Mother Teresa began looking around for new headquarters for her fledgling order. She and the nuns "stormed heaven" with constant prayers.

An answer to their prayers came in the form of a mysterious man who led Mother Teresa to a spacious three-story building on Lower Circular Road and introduced her to the owner. The Muslim owner was surprised that anyone knew he was planning to sell his home, for he had told only his wife. He sold Mother Teresa the home for a fraction of its value, pleased that he could contribute to the work of the Missionaries of Charity.

In February 1953, nearly thirty Missionaries of Charity moved into their new home, the order's motherhouse, at 54A Lower Circular Road. They furnished the motherhouse sparingly, without comforts or modern conveniences such as stoves, air conditioners, washing machines, or electric fans. "I do not want them," Mother Teresa said, "the poor we serve have none."

The nuns washed clothes by hand and prepared food for themselves and the poor over charcoal fires. Mother Teresa said, "Poverty is necessary because we are working with the poor. When they complain about the food, we can say, 'We eat the same.' They say, 'It was so hot last night, we could not sleep.' We can reply, 'We also felt very hot.' The poor have to wash for themselves, go barefoot; we do the same."

Many of the city's poor thronged at the entrance of the motherhouse, where the nuns operated a soup kitchen. The nuns also traveled to Calcutta's poorest neighborhoods by foot or on public transportation. They distributed food and medicine and instructed people about hygiene.

Mother Teresa refused to install a phone line at the motherhouse. After all, she wondered, how many people would the price of telephone service feed? When she realized it would help her mission, however, she reluctantly allowed one phone.

Although the food the nuns ate was inexpensive and plain, Mother Teresa followed the advice of Mother Dengal and insisted that her nuns be well fed.

"Mother made us eat plenty," said Sister Bernard, one of the first to join the new order. "[She] was always afraid that we might get TB [tuberculosis] or things like that. But we kept good health."

Mother Teresa was pleased to receive new novices as long as they met her strict requirements. They had to live without income, personal possessions, or lives outside the order. All that they had was to be given to God and to the poor. Their worldly possessions consisted of three saris, a rosary (a string of beads used in counting prayers), a Bible, a copy of the order's constitution, and a bucket for washing. They were not allowed to accept anything—not even a cup of tea or a glass of water—from anyone. Mother Teresa often explained that the poor, wanting to thank her nuns for their service, might offer something they could not afford to give. By not accepting anything from anyone—rich or poor—the nuns would offend no one.

Mother Teresa expected her nuns to serve the poor willingly and happily and always with a smile on their face—as she herself had been doing for several years. She wanted them to wash sores and wounds, change bedpans, and mop up urine and vomit with the same respect and reverence as if they were praying to God. "If you don't have the zeal to help the poor, to take good care of the lepers, then [you] should pack up and go home," Mother Teresa told a group of novices. "No need to stay."

Missionaries of Charity had to give up links with their

families, as the Catholic Church had required Mother Teresa to do—but they were allowed home visits once every ten years or if a family member was dying.

Each year on the tenth of September, the Missionaries of Charity celebrated "Inspiration Day," the day Mother Teresa had received her "call within her call." They also celebrated the order's anniversary on the seventh of October.

Steadfast in her confidence that God would provide, Mother Teresa refused regular financial support from the Indian government and the Catholic Church. Although Mother Teresa continued to write her begging letters and to make begging trips, she refused fundraising done on her behalf, taking only direct donations. "Money, I never give it a thought," she said. "It always comes. We do all our work for our Lord. He must look after us."

Donations did come. When people wanted to donate funds to the organization, Mother Teresa was so persuasive and intense that she often convinced them to give more than they first intended. She would tell people, "I don't want your money from abundance, I don't want to relieve your conscience, but I want you to give until it hurts: to give because you want to share the poverty and suffering of our poor." People gave more to the Missionaries of Charity than to other charities because Mother Teresa appealed to their conscience. People also knew that their donations would go directly to helping the poor.

With Mother Teresa at the helm, the Missionaries of Charity began to develop new ways to help as many of Calcutta's poor as they could. Every day in Calcutta, people lay dying in the gutters, alone and rejected, rats gnawing on their bodies. One day in 1954, Mother Teresa found a woman dying in a gutter. After having to beg doctors at a local hospital to help the woman in her last hours, Mother Teresa resolved to find a building to give the poor a place to die with dignity. She spread the word that she wanted the dying to die secure in the knowledge that they were loved by the Missionaries of Charity.

The city of Calcutta soon donated a building located next to a Hindu temple in the city's Kalighat district. Kalighat was a place of holy importance. Each year, Hindus made pilgrimages there to pay homage to the goddess Kali and to visit the sacred waters of the nearby Ganges River. For many years, these Hindu pilgrims stayed in the building that the city had just donated to Mother Teresa. The Missionaries of Charity renamed it *Nirmal Hriday* (Place of the Immaculate Heart). The building became the mission's home for the dying. The nuns would walk through the streets of Calcutta picking up people dying from malnutrition and disease and bring them to Nirmal Hriday, where the nuns washed and fed them and put them in beds. The building's two huge rooms had rows of cots or mattresses on the floor to accommodate the many new people brought in each day.

"We have never had to turn anybody away because there has always been one more bed, one more plate of rice, one more blanket to cover," Mother Teresa said. It was very important to her that the dying felt loved and comfortable in their last moments on earth.

Mother Teresa faced a series of challenges soon after Nirmal Hriday opened. Some Hindus opposed a house of death located so close to their sacred temple. They claimed the home was an insult to their belief that death is an unclean condition. Protesters threw stones at the building and threatened to storm it unless it was

A Hindu man prays at the Kali temple, next to Mother Teresa's home for the dying.

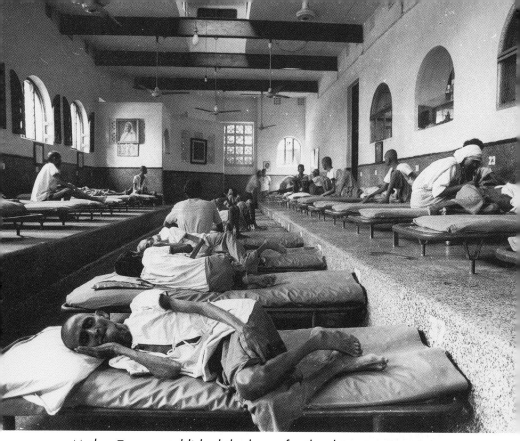

Mother Teresa established the home for the dying to give poor people a place to die with dignity.

closed down. The Missionaries of Charity bravely continued working. Calcutta city officials were brought in to control the growing and angry crowds. These officials toured Nirmal Hriday and realized that the nuns were caring for people of all religions and burying each one in the tradition of his or her own religion. They told the crowd that until someone else stepped in to do the work of Mother Teresa, Nirmal Hriday would remain open.

Led by Mother Teresa, the nuns took on their next challenge. In 1955, they expanded their care of poor

Mother Teresa was undaunted by protests from Hindu pilgrims calling for her to close Nirmal Hriday.

children by opening *Shishu Bhavan* (Children's Home), a facility to care for orphans and children with disabilities. In a nation where families faced the daily prospect of starvation, it was not unusual for parents to abandon their children if they could not care for them. The Missionaries of Charity found these children in the streets and brought them to Shishu Bhavan. After Shishu Bhavan became well established, parents, social workers, and police officers began bringing abandoned and orphaned children there, knowing that the nuns would care for them and find them new homes.

Once Shishu Bhavan was established, Mother Teresa turned her attention to India's two million leprosy patients. Because leprosy was a disease surrounded by superstition and fear, Mother Teresa had trouble convincing Calcutta city officials to allow her to open a leprosy clinic in the city. Although leprosy can only be spread by contact with an open wound, many people did not know or believe this. When people, rich or poor, contracted leprosy, they were usually thrown out of their homes or taken to the few established leper colonies, where they lived and worked apart from the rest of the world.

Shishu Bhavan *(Children's Home) is a bright and cheery place where children laugh and play.*

Determined not to walk away from a challenge, Mother Teresa found a way to treat the many leprosy patients who she felt needed her. She used a large corporate donation and an ambulance delivered from the United States to start a mobile leper clinic. This clinic took medical supplies to government-approved leprosy centers where the nuns treated hundreds of patients at once. With the help of volunteers, Mother Teresa established the Leprosy Fund and Leprosy Day, challenging people to "touch a leper with your compassion."

This girl, a victim of leprosy, was treated at a leper colony in India.

In just a few years, Mother Teresa had evolved from a leader within the schools of Loreto to a leader in Calcutta. She was entirely focused on serving God through serving the poor. This belief gave her the remarkable energy, strength, and compassion for which she was becoming known. She continued to seek even more ways to help those in need.

During a visit to India, Pope Paul VI gave Mother Teresa a white Lincoln Continental limousine in which he had been driven. She raffled the car and used the $100,000 proceeds to start *Shanti Nagar* (Place of Peace), a leper colony built on land donated by the Indian government. Located six hours from Calcutta, Shanti Nagar was a place where people with leprosy could live, work, and receive medical treatment for their illness. Patients were almost totally self-sufficient. They grew their own food, wove baskets, and made other crafts to sell. The colony flourished.

While the Missionaries of Charity were only treating a small percentage of India's poor, dying, and abandoned, Mother Teresa believed her work could reach all who needed her care. "So wonderful is the way of God," she said. "We will eventually get to them all."

Mother Teresa greets Prince Charles during his visit to Shishu Bhavan.

Chapter NINE

A MISSION GROWS

THE **1960**S MARKED THE BEGINNING OF NATIONAL and international recognition for Mother Teresa, who was then in her fifties. In 1962, her work earned her the Order of the Lotus award from the Indian government and the Magsaysay award from a partnership of Asian nations. Other awards followed, including the American Good Samaritan Award, the Templeton Award for Progress in Religion, and the Pope John XXIII Peace Prize. These prizes were often accompanied by significant cash awards, which Mother Teresa always accepted for the poor she served and funneled into her growing missions. She refused to take credit for the humanitarian work she conducted in the name of God. "I am like a little pencil in God's hand," she often said. "He does the thinking. He does the writing. The pencil has only to be allowed to be used."

In 1960, Mother Teresa left India for the first time in over thirty years. She traveled to Europe and to the United States, where she had been invited to speak at a conference for Catholic women. She wanted to raise people's awareness of poverty in their own country. "Most of the time people don't even know the existence of the poor. We look and we don't see. . . . You can find Calcutta all over the world, if you have eyes to see," she said.

While in Italy, Mother Teresa was reunited with her brother, Lazar. Having once questioned his sister's choice to leave home and become a nun, he now wholeheartedly supported her. "It can be truly said that she is a commandant of a unit or an entire fleet," he said. "Her strength of will is unbelievable, like our mother's."

Lazar introduced his humanitarian sister to his wife and daughter. The reunion was tempered with sadness, however. Drana and Age were still living as virtual prisoners in Albania. Despite Mother Teresa's repeated requests to enter Albania, the country's Communist government did not want a religious figure such as Mother Teresa to enter the country. Many influential people, including Indian Prime Minister Indira Gandhi, petitioned the Albanian government on Mother Teresa's behalf, but with no success.

Despite her own grief, Mother Teresa pushed on

with her work back in India. In the early 1960s, the Missionaries of Charity began opening convents, homes for the dying, and orphanages throughout India. In 1963, to help the Missionaries of Charity expand their work, the archbishop of Calcutta gave Mother Teresa permission to begin the Missionary Brothers of Charity. This allowed priests to assist in work done by Mother Teresa's nuns.

In 1965, to mark the Missionaries of Charity's fifteenth anniversary, Pope Paul VI gave the order permission to open homes outside India, sparking a period of rapid expansion for the Missionaries of Charity. Upon the invitation of local Catholic bishops, Mother Teresa opened the first international Missionaries of Charity home in Venezuela, and then several more in other South American countries. In 1968, she opened a home in Rome, Italy, and then moved on to Tanzania, a country in East Africa.

Although the Catholic Church was run by a hierarchy of male priests who made all the important decisions, even for convents headed by a mother superior, Mother Teresa insisted that she would not allow priest interference. Priests were welcome to say mass, give holy communion, and hear confession, but the running of her order—and all decisions—would be left to Mother Teresa and her nuns. Each of the Missionaries of Charity homes had a mother superior who reported to a regional supervisor who in turn reported to one of four councillors-general.

As the number of her missions throughout the world grew, the donations Mother Teresa accepted were distributed among many Missionaries of Charity programs. In 1969, Pope Paul VI allowed Mother Teresa's Co-Workers—a network of lay people helping Mother Teresa and her nuns—to be officially recognized as part of the Missionaries of Charity. The Co-Workers were made up of people of all faiths, races, and backgrounds who were determined to help Mother Teresa serve the poor. Begun informally in Calcutta by a British woman, Ann Blaikie, the work of ordinary citizens grew into an organized effort to help Mother

Pope Paul VI blesses Mother Teresa.

Teresa. Co-Workers, who lived all over the world, would keep in touch through an international newsletter. As the Co-Workers became an increasingly important part of the Missionaries of Charity, Mother Teresa referred to them as her second self.

By 1970, more than a thousand nuns had joined the Missionaries of Charity from all over the world. Young girls flocked to Mother Teresa because they wanted to help the sick and the suffering. With the extensive network of brothers and Co-Workers, Mother Teresa's organization was helping poor people in nearly one hundred countries.

As Mother Teresa and the Missionaries of Charity gained international recognition, journalists eagerly questioned Mother Teresa about herself. When asked about her early life, Mother Teresa told them only that she had had a happy childhood. Other personal questions she deftly turned around as an opportunity to discuss the poor and her work. She wasn't about to waste a media opportunity talking about herself when her important work could be broadcast to the world.

On July 12, 1972, Mother Teresa received sad news from Lazar. Their beloved mother had died in Albania. Drana's last wish to see her youngest daughter had not been granted. Two years later, Age died alone in Albania. Mother Teresa did not outwardly express her grief, believing that God's plan was to reunite the Bojaxhiu family in heaven.

On October 17, 1979, seven years after Drana's death,

one of the world's greatest honors was bestowed on sixty-nine-year-old Mother Teresa. After being nominated three times earlier, Mother Teresa was awarded the prestigious Nobel Peace Prize and became only the sixth woman to receive the award in its seventy-eight-year history. When reporters descended on the motherhouse at 54A Lower Circular Road, Mother Teresa told them, "I accept the prize in the name of the poor." As the media buzzed around the convent, getting in the way of Mother Teresa's work, she said, "I am going to hide somewhere." Even the world's most prestigious prize would not distract her from her work.

In December, Mother Teresa traveled to Oslo, Norway, with two Missionaries of Charity, Sisters Agnes and Gertrude, to accept the prize from Norway's King Olaf V. The city was decorated for the festivities. Pictures of Mother Teresa and tributes to her hung from windows and street signs. Upon her arrival, she astounded the world by requesting that the prize committee cancel the traditional banquet and instead donate the funds to the Missionaries of Charity. Mother Teresa did not like to see money wasted on frivolities when all over the world people were starving. She used the $192,000 Nobel Peace Prize cash allotment, $6,000 from the canceled banquet, $72,000 from private Norwegian donations, and funds raised by Norwegian schoolchildren to build homes for the poor in India.

At the awards ceremony, Mother Teresa—dressed in

In 1979, Mother Teresa received the prestigious Nobel Peace Prize in Oslo, Norway.

her simple blue and white sari—told the audience of influential world citizens, "Our poor people are great people, a very lovable people. . . . We need to tell the poor that they are somebody to us, that they, too, have been created by the same loving hand of God, to love and be loved." She also used the international forum to speak against abortion. "To me the nations with legalized abortion are the poorest nations," she told the audience. "If a mother can kill her own child, what will prevent us from killing one another?"

By the time Mother Teresa had won this prestigious prize, her work had become known throughout the world. In 1979, the Missionaries of Charity boasted almost 2,000 nuns and 120,000 Co-Workers toiling in orphanages, youth homes, shelters, hospitals, and leper colonies around the world. Often, national leaders asked Mother Teresa to open a convent in their country.

The determined Mother Teresa knew how to use the press to her advantage. While traveling in South America, she once asked a top government official, on camera, for an empty building she had seen on the ride from the airport. With a news crew anxiously awaiting his reply, how could the official refuse? Donors knew that if they gave money to the Missionaries of Charity, they would be publicly praised and acknowledged.

The year that Mother Teresa was awarded the Nobel Peace Prize, India suffered a terrible drought. Overwhelming food shortages again plagued the nation, and even emergency food supplies were not enough to feed the starving masses. More than thirty years after Mother Teresa began her work with the poor, India still needed her desperately.

Mother Teresa ushered in the 1980s with a return visit to Skopje to open a Missionaries of Charity home. During Mother Teresa's long absence, Skopje had become a part of the country of Yugoslavia. "I found Skopje very changed," Mother Teresa said, "but it continued to be my Skopje, where I had spent my childhood with my family and where I was happy. . . . I always carry in my heart the people of Skopje and Albania."

The "Saint of the Gutters," as people around the world had begun calling Mother Teresa, was in great demand as a lecturer. She dutifully traveled more than ever and was sometimes away from the motherhouse for ten months of the year. Wherever she went, she distributed small cards with simple prayers or religious poems printed on them. Mother Teresa joked that these were her business cards. She hoped to persuade people to serve the poor in their own country—and, of course, she wanted them to donate money to the Missionaries of Charity. In each country, she visited the poor on the streets or in shelters. Mother Teresa's favorite greeting to anyone, wealthy or poor, was to hold a person's head in her hands and touch her forehead to theirs. She felt she connected with people by touching them.

As the Missionaries of Charity grew, it became a multibillion-dollar organization, with most of its worth in buildings that had been donated. As was typical of Mother Teresa, she and her nuns found additional outlets for their work. There seemed to be no end to the demand for their services. In addition to tending to hungry, ill, dying, and orphaned people, and teaching in schools, the Missionaries of Charity began to help runaways and recovering drug addicts and alcoholics. "When there are no more poor, no more hungry, no more lepers—then we will retire to our convent and give ourselves entirely to pray," Mother Teresa said, "but I hardly think that time will come."

But the hardworking and famous nun, well into her seventies, began to show signs of aging. In 1983,

Mother Teresa suffered a severe heart attack and was advised by her doctors to slow down. Instead, she worked as vigorously as ever. "I've never said no to Jesus," she said, "and I'm not going to begin now. Every day you have to say yes."

Mother Teresa went wherever help was needed. In 1982, during a conflict between Lebanon and neighboring Israel, Mother Teresa traveled to Lebanon's capital, Beirut. She tried to convince government and Red Cross officials to let her into West Beirut to tend to disabled children left in hospitals bombed during

Fans around the world flocked to touch their beloved Mother Teresa.

Mother Teresa greets two of the children she rescued from a bombed Lebanese hospital in 1982.

the conflict. Skeptical officials doubted that the seventy-two-year-old nun could offer anything but prayers until terms of a cease-fire were negotiated, and they would not let her cross into the war-ravaged section.

Resigned that praying was the only way to reach those who needed her care, Mother Teresa asked God for a cease-fire between Lebanon and Israel. The next day a cease-fire was announced. Accompanied by Red Cross relief workers and four ambulances, Mother Teresa hurried into West Beirut, through bombed streets, and past piles of wreckage and debris. With her usual effectiveness, Mother Teresa scooped up patients and whisked them to a Missionaries of Charity home in East Beirut, where her nuns were waiting to care for them. One Red Cross worker remarked, "What stunned everyone was her energy and efficiency. She saw the problem, fell to her knees and prayed for a few seconds and then she was rattling off a list of supplies she needed."

Mother Teresa was invited to lecture throughout the world. She was especially outspoken on the issue of abortion.

Chapter **TEN**

CONTROVERSY

AS MOTHER TERESA'S WORK SPREAD AROUND THE world, so did criticism against her. Some still questioned her motives for helping the poor, believing that she was trying to convert people to Christianity. Mother Teresa answered these people by saying, "I convert you to be a better Hindu, a better Catholic, a better Muslim . . . or Buddhist."

Mother Teresa was also criticized by some people in the medical profession. They argued that many of the nuns were not properly trained in medicine, did not keep sterile facilities, and spent money intended for medications on opening new homes. They also quarreled with Mother Teresa's insistence that, to save money, syringes and needles be reused on different people.

Another major criticism lodged against Mother Teresa was that she never made attempts to solve the causes of poverty, but only ministered to its effects. Critics argued that the money given to the Missionaries of Charity would be better spent on instructing poor people in developing countries in areas of birth control, personal hygiene, and the importance of education and job training. Some people believed that Mother Teresa should have used her power and influence with world leaders to develop programs to change the lives of the poor, not just step in with temporary measures to relieve day-to-day suffering.

But it was Mother Teresa's stance on abortion and birth control that generated the most criticism. With so many developing countries—including India—dangerously overpopulated, her critics were outraged by her very vocal belief that a family could never have too many children, regardless of its financial situation. Mother Teresa advocated having large families despite the fact that a majority of the people the Missionaries of Charity helped were so poor that they could barely support one child, much less several. While the Indian government promoted smaller families and birth control, Mother Teresa strongly discouraged artificial contraception, arguing that only God should decide when a life is conceived. The Missionaries of Charity promoted natural family planning, a method organized around the time during a woman's menstrual cycle when she can become pregnant. But this method was often out of reach of the people the Missionaries of Charity served because following the system required the ability to read, write, and keep accurate time records. Mother Teresa opposed abortion in any instance— even in cases of rape, child molestation, or incest— another stance which drew sharp criticism from around the world.

Although Mother Teresa always maintained that she was not a political figure, she still tried to influence political leaders to make laws against abortion. Mother Teresa took every opportunity to speak out against abortion—during her many public appearances, in private meetings with world leaders, or in numerous letters she sent to governments in foreign countries. In one letter she wrote, "I feel God wants me to appeal to you on behalf of the unborn child. . . . The only one who has the right to take life is the One who created it. Nobody else has that right. I am sure that deep down in your heart, you know that the unborn child is a human being, loved by God. I am offering my prayers for your country, that as a nation, you will always choose to respect and love the gift of life in every individual."

Mother Teresa's alternative to abortion was adoption. "We have sent word to all the clinics and hospitals, do not destroy the child, we will take the child," Mother Teresa said. "We are fighting abortion by adoption." This stance also drew criticism. Critics believed that if the Missionaries of Charity did not oppose birth

The Missionaries of Charity have placed thousands of babies abandoned by their birth parents with families around the world.

control, there would be little need for abortion or adoption. Others did not like the fact that children in the care of the Missionaries of Charity often were adopted out of their native countries and placed with families of different races. Mother Teresa also was criticized for refusing to let couples who had used artificial birth control methods adopt children cared for by the Missionaries of Charity.

Regardless of the criticism, Mother Teresa continued

the work that she had been called by God to do. "I am not trying to change anything," she told her critics. "I am only trying to live my love." In 1990 alone, Mother Teresa and her Missionaries of Charity fed more than five hundred thousand families, taught twenty thousand children in 124 schools, and cared for ninety thousand leprosy patients in more than one hundred countries.

As Mother Teresa entered her eighties, she became increasingly ill and frail with heart disease. She was hospitalized twice during 1988 and 1989 and received

In the motherhouse, Missionaries of Charity sing "Happy Birthday" to the eighty-year-old Mother Teresa.

a pacemaker to help control her heart ailment. By 1990, she felt she was too ill to continue running her order, and in April she retired. Still she continued lecturing and traveling to her Missionaries of Charity convents around the world. Air India, after declining her tongue-in-cheek offer to work as a stewardess in exchange for airfare, had given Mother Teresa and her nuns free passage anywhere the airline flew.

But within five months of her retirement, it was obvious that the order still needed Mother Teresa. The Missionaries of Charity had failed to elect a replacement, and in September Mother Teresa was reelected as the order's superior general. Old, sick, and frail, she once again assumed the role she had spent more than half her life playing. As the world watched Mother Teresa take the helm again, religious and political leaders worried about the future of the Missionaries of Charity. The order seemed unable to function without Mother Teresa.

Ever confident that God would provide for the Missionaries of Charity, Mother Teresa did not worry about who would take her place upon her death. "Just as God has found me, he will find somebody else. The work is God's work, and he will see to it," she said.

Rejecting her doctors' repeated advice to slow down, Mother Teresa continued to travel extensively and collapsed twice between 1991 and 1993. Both times she was hospitalized. "I have all eternity to rest and there is so much still to do," she said. "Life is not worth living unless it is lived for others."

As she continued to travel, she became more and more frail, breaking her collarbone and a foot in 1996. Determined not to let her ailments slow her down, Mother Teresa traveled in a wheelchair and was present at the opening of the 565th Missionaries of Charity home, in Wales.

For the next year, she was in and out of the hospital suffering from heart problems and malaria. Resigned to the fact that they would soon lose their beloved Mother, the Missionaries of Charity elected a new superior general. On March 13, 1997, they elected Sister

Sister Nirmala, left, *replaced Mother Teresa as the superior general of the Missionaries of Charity.*

Nirmala, a sixty-three-year-old nun who had been with the order for nearly forty years. The shy, reserved woman had been at Mother Teresa's side during many overseas trips and was much respected. As a tribute to the beloved Mother Teresa, Sister Nirmala maintained that there was only one Mother. Sister Nirmala would still be known as Sister.

People around the world continued to worry about the future of the Missionaries of Charity, however. Mother

Mother Teresa had many famous friends. She and Princess Diana supported some of the same causes.

Mother Teresa participates in a ceremony at the Vatican, the center of the Catholic Church, in Rome.

Teresa had kept her nuns fairly isolated since the founding of her order. When reporters and news crews attempted to interview the nuns, they shyly backed away. The attention made them uncomfortable.

To honor the eighty-six-year-old nun, the United States Congress in 1996 awarded Mother Teresa the Congressional Medal of Honor and gave her an honorary U.S. citizenship, something awarded to only four other individuals in the nation's two-hundred-year history.

Being recognized with an honorary citizenship seemed fitting for a woman who considered herself a citizen of the world. "By blood and origin I am an Albanian," she once said. "My citizenship is Indian. I am a Catholic nun. As to my calling, I belong to all the world. As to my heart, I belong entirely to the heart of Jesus."

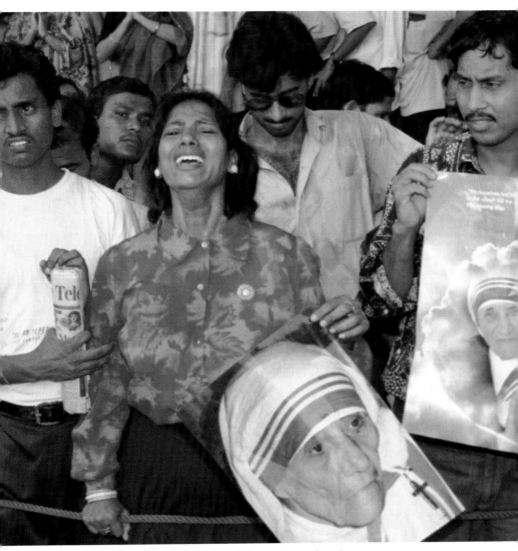

Thousands of mourners lined the streets of Calcutta to say a final farewell to Mother Teresa during her funeral procession.

Chapter ELEVEN

THE DEATH OF A SAINT

WHEN THE MISSIONARIES OF CHARITY RANG THE bells at 54A Lower Circular Road, Calcutta, on September 6, 1997, they were telling the world that it had lost one of its most beloved figures. Mother Teresa, born Agnes Gonxha Bojaxhiu, had died of heart failure in the motherhouse at the age of eighty-seven. A crowd of thousands quickly gathered around the Missionaries of Charity headquarters, grieving at the news of her death.

Indian citizens—Christians, Hindus, Muslims, and others—came from across the region to say good-bye to Mother Teresa. One man said, "We think of Mother not as a Christian but simply as Mother. She was just the Mother of us all." Missionaries of Charity journeyed to the motherhouse from around the world to say a final prayer for their leader.

On the day of Mother Teresa's funeral, thousands of mourners gathered in Calcutta and stood in long lines to get a glimpse of the body during the public viewing. As the funeral procession moved slowly through the streets of Calcutta, hundreds of thousands of mourners lined the streets, dropping flower petals, holding up her picture, and chanting prayers.

Indian officials arranged a state funeral, held in an indoor sports stadium to accommodate the crowd. Services were attended by many world leaders, including the president of Albania. Representatives from India's many religious institutions blessed the nun who had meant so much to their country. Mother Teresa was buried on the grounds of the motherhouse.

As the world said good-bye to Mother Teresa, many wondered if Pope John Paul II would declare Mother Teresa a saint, a long and complex process. Mother Teresa's lifelong devotion to the poor had earned her the name "living saint," and people worldwide believed she was deserving of sainthood. The complex process of canonization, or declaring sainthood, can last for fifty to one hundred years. It involves investigation and prayer, and usually does not begin until at least five years after the person's death. But as supreme leader of the Catholic Church, Pope John Paul II, a great admirer of Mother Teresa, has the power to declare her a saint at any time.

Regardless of Mother Teresa's status as a saint, the fact remains that her work has touched the lives of millions of people worldwide. In 1998, there were more than forty-five hundred Missionaries of Charity nuns with more than 550 centers in 126 countries. As the world's problems have grown, so have the Missionaries of Charity services. The organization has begun to care for AIDS patients and battered women and gives employment counseling to the unemployed. Some people believe that as Sister Nirmala ushers in a new era for the Missionaries of Charity, the organization will answer some of its critics and work to address the causes of poverty.

Mother Teresa's calling from God—to serve the poorest of the poor—changed many lives and inspired the world. She was a powerful woman in a church whose leaders are men; a woman who, in her efforts to serve the poor, formed influential friendships and liaisons with some of the world's most celebrated and important figures. But to the citizens of the world's poorest nations, she was simply Mother, a woman who cared deeply for the destitute and who devoted her life to easing their suffering. For millions of people, Mother Teresa has become a lasting symbol of the power of love. "Love has to be put into action," she often said. From her days in Skopje until her death, Mother Teresa lived true to that motto, inspiring thousands by her example.

FOR FURTHER READING

Albania in Pictures. Minneapolis: Lerner Publications Company, 1995.

Beckett, Wendy. *Sister Wendy's Book of Saints.* New York: Dorling Kindersley, 1998.

Bowker, John. *World Religions.* New York: Dorling Kindersley, 1997.

India in Pictures. Minneapolis: Lerner Publications Company, 1989.

McBrien, Richard P., ed. *Encyclopedia of Catholicism.* San Francisco: Harper San Francisco, 1995.

Rice, Tanya. *The Life and Times of Mother Teresa.* Philadelphia: Chelsea House, 1998.

Royle, Roger, and Gary Woods. *Mother Teresa: A Life in Pictures.* San Francisco: Harper San Francisco, 1992.

SOURCES

11–12 Mother Teresa, *My Life for the Poor* (San Francisco: Harper & Row, 1997), 3.

12 David Porter, *Mother Teresa: The Early Years* (Grand Rapids, Mich.: William B. Eerdmans, 1986), 24.

12 Teresa, *My Life,* 4.

21 Ibid., 2, 4.

24 Porter, *Mother Teresa,* 24.

26 Teresa, *My Life,* 5.

28 Anne Sebba, *Mother Teresa: Beyond the Image* (New York: Doubleday, 1997), 19.

28 Lush Gjergji, *Mother Teresa: Her Life, Her Works* (Hyde Park, NY: New City Press, 1990), 23.

28 Teresa, *My Life,* 4.

29 Ibid.

29 Navin Chawla, *Mother Teresa: The Authorized Biography* (Rockport, Mass.: Element Books, 1996), 5.

29 Sebba, *Mother Teresa,* 20.

31–32 Porter, *Mother Teresa,* 32.

32 Ibid.

35 Ibid., 37.

37 Ibid., 38.

41 Ibid., 40–41.

42 Ibid., 29.

43 Teresa, *My Life,* 5–6.

45 Porter, *Mother Teresa,* 47.

45 Teresa, *My Life,* 6.

48 Chawla, *Mother Teresa,* 54.

50 Teresa, *My Life,* 7.

52 Chawla, *Mother Teresa,* 21.

53 Desmond Doig, *Mother Teresa: Her People and Her Work* (New York: Harper & Row, 1976), 64.

53 Teresa, *My Life,* 9.

56 Ibid., 14.

57 Ibid., 10.

61–62 Eileen Egan, *Such a Vision of the Street* (New York: Doubleday, 1985), 38.

63   Sebba, *Mother Teresa,* 53–54.

64   Teresa, *My Life,* 11.

64   Ibid., 39.

64–65   Ibid., 13.

65   Ibid., 15.

66   Gjergji, *Mother Teresa,* 15.

68   Porter, *Mother Teresa,* 80.

68   Mother Teresa, *No Greater Love* (Novato, Ca.: New World Library, 1997), 98.

69   Doig, *Mother Teresa,* 80.

69   *Mother Teresa,* prod. and dir. Anne Petrie, 82 min., Petrie Productions, Inc., 1987, videocassette.

70   Chawla, *Mother Teresa,* 74.

70   Teresa, *My Life,* 59.

72   Ibid., 53.

77   Kathryn Spink, *The Miracle of Love. Mother Teresa of Calcutta, Her Missionaries of Charity, and Her Co-Workers* (New York: Harper & Row), 62.

79–80   Subir Bhaumik, Meenakshi Ganguly, and Tim McGirk, "Seeker of Souls," *Time,* September 17, 1997, 80.

80   Petrie, *Mother Teresa,* videocassette.

80   Gjergji, *Mother Teresa,* 32.

84   Sebba, *Mother Teresa,* 100.

84   Frank J. Prial, "Mother Teresa of Calcutta Wins Peace Prize," *New York Times,* October 18, 1979, A14.

85   Associated Press, "Mother Teresa, Receiving Nobel, Assails Abortion," *New York Times,* December 11, 1979, A3.

85   Gjergji, *Mother Teresa,* 138.

86   Teresa, *My life,* 3.

87   Porter, *Mother Teresa,* 98.

88   Petrie, *Mother Teresa,* videocassette.

89   Sebba, *Mother Teresa,* 112.

91   Chawla, *Mother Teresa,* 73.

93   "Mother Teresa's Letter to the People of Africa," n.d., http://www.hli.org/issues/reports/samessg.html> (31 August 1998).

93   Petrie, *Mother Teresa,* videocassette.

   95   Marci McDonald, "Death of a Saint," *Macleans,*
         September 15, 1997, 22.
   96   Chawla, *Mother Teresa,* 207.
   96   Sarah Gibbings, "Mother Teresa's Message to Diana,"
         Good Housekeeping, December 1990, 246.
   99   Woodward, "Little Sister," 70.
101–102   Ibid., 25.
  103   Petrie, *Mother Teresa,* videocassette.

BIBLIOGRAPHY

BOOKS

The Bible, Revised Standard Version. New York: American Bible Society, 1973.

Bradnock, Robert and Roma Bradnock, eds. *India Handbook.* Chicago: Passport Books, 1995.

Chawla, Navin. *Mother Teresa: The Authorized Biography.* Rockport, Mass.: Element Books, 1996.

Clucas, Joan G. *Mother Teresa.* New York: Chelsea House, 1988.

Doig, Desmond. *Mother Teresa: Her People and Her Work.* New York: Harper & Row, 1976.

Egan, Eileen. *Such a Vision of the Street.* New York: Doubleday, 1985.

Gjergji, Lush. *Mother Teresa: Her Life, Her Works.* Hyde Park, NY: New City Press, 1990.

Johnson, Otto, ed. *1996 Information Please Almanac.* Boston: Houghton Mifflin Company, 1996.

Kendall, Patricia C. *Come with Me to India: A Quest for Truth among Peoples and Problems.* New York: Charles Scribner's Sons, 1931.

Le Joly, Edward. *Mother Teresa of Calcutta.* San Francisco: Harper & Row, 1977.

Moorhouse, Geoffrey. *Calcutta.* New York: Harcourt Brace Jovanovich, Inc., 1971.

Porter, David. *Mother Teresa: The Early Years.* Grand Rapids, Mich.: William B. Eerdmans, 1986.

Sebba, Anne. *Mother Teresa: Beyond the Image.* New York: Doubleday, 1997.

Spink, Kathryn. *The Miracle of Love: Mother Teresa of Calcutta, Her Missionaries of Charity, and Her Co-Workers.* New York: Harper & Row, 1981.

Teresa, Mother. *My Life for the Poor.* Edited by José Luis González-Balado and Janet N. Playfoot. San Francisco: Harper & Row, 1985.

Ibid. *No Greater Love.* Novato, Ca.: New World Library, 1997.

Magazines and Newspaper Articles

Bhaumik, Subir, Meenakshi Ganguly and Tim McGirk. "Seeker of Souls." *Time*, September 17, 1997, 79–84.

Cooper, Kenneth J. "Throngs in Calcutta Mourn Mother Teresa." *The Washington Post*, September 7, 1997, A19.

Desmond, Edward W. "Interview: A Pencil in the Hand of God." *Time*, December 4, 1989, 12–13.

Gibbings, Sarah. "Mother Teresa's Message to Diana." *Good Housekeeping*, December 1990, 246.

Hazarika, Sanjoy. "Gas Leak in India Kills at Least 410 in City of Bhopal." *The New York Times*, December 3, 1984, A1, A8.

Kaufman, Michael T. "India is Combating Effects of Drought." *New York Times*, December 10, 1979, A2.

McDonald, Marci. "Death of a 'Saint.'" *Macleans*, September 15, 1997, 22–25.

New York Times Service. "Christianity Long in India." *Richmond Times-Dispatch*, September 15, 1997, A8.

Noonan, Peggy. "A Combatant in the World." *Time*, September 15, 1997, 84.

Scripps Howard News Service. "Tiny Nun Biggest Story in Religion," *Richmond Times-Dispatch*, December 27, 1997, B6.

Suralya, Jug. "First Lady of Calcutta." *Far Eastern Economic Review*, March 25, 1993, 44.

Woodward, Kenneth L. "Little Sister of the Poor." *Newsweek*, September 15, 1997, 70–74.

Ibid. "Requiem for a Saint." *Newsweek*, September 22, 1997, 22–36.

Electronic Media

"Mother Teresa: Her Talks." n.d. <http://www.tisv.be/mt/talk.htm> (31 August 1998).

"Remembering Mother Teresa of Calcutta.," n.d. <http://www.qas.org/mompics.htm> (31 August 1998).

Teresa, Mother. *Mother Teresa*. Produced and directed by Anne Petrie. 82 min. Petrie Productions, Inc., 1987. Videocassette.

Other

United States Congress, Public Law 104–218, October 1, 1996.

United States Congress, Public Law 105–16, June, 1997.

INDEX

ABOUT THE AUTHOR

Amy Ruth is a writer in Williamsburg, Virginia, and teaches college composition. She has a master's degree in journalism from the University of Iowa and writes regularly for magazines and newspapers. She and her writer/photographer husband, Jim Meisner, often collaborate on projects. This is her third book for young people.

PHOTO ACKNOWLEDGMENTS

AP/Wide World Photos pp. 62, 85, 89, 90, 95; © Catholic News Service/Wiechec, p.2; © Catholic News Service/Arturo Mari, p. 99; Dinodia Picture Agency/SOA, p.54; Dinodia Picture Agency/Rajesh Vora, p.76; Dinodia Picture Agency, p.97; Drita Publishing/ Editrice VELAR, pp. 6, 9, 16, 20, 22, 25, 30, 34, 36; The Illustrated London News Picture Library, p.38; Jim Meisner, p. 112; Mirror Syndication International, p. 74; Reuters/Mike Segar/Archive Photos, p. 98; Reuters/Joy Shaw/Archive Photos, p. 100; Reuters/ Sunil Malhotra/ Archive Photos, p. 107; © Trip/H. Rogers, p. 72; UPI/Corbis-Bettman pp. 13, 14, 27, 51, 52, 57, 78, 82, 88, 94; Laura Westlund, pp. 10, 11, 39; Gary Woods pp. 42,46, 61, 66, 73, 75. Front cover photograph: UPI/ Corbis-Bettman. Back cover photograph: Drita Publishing/Editrice VELAR.